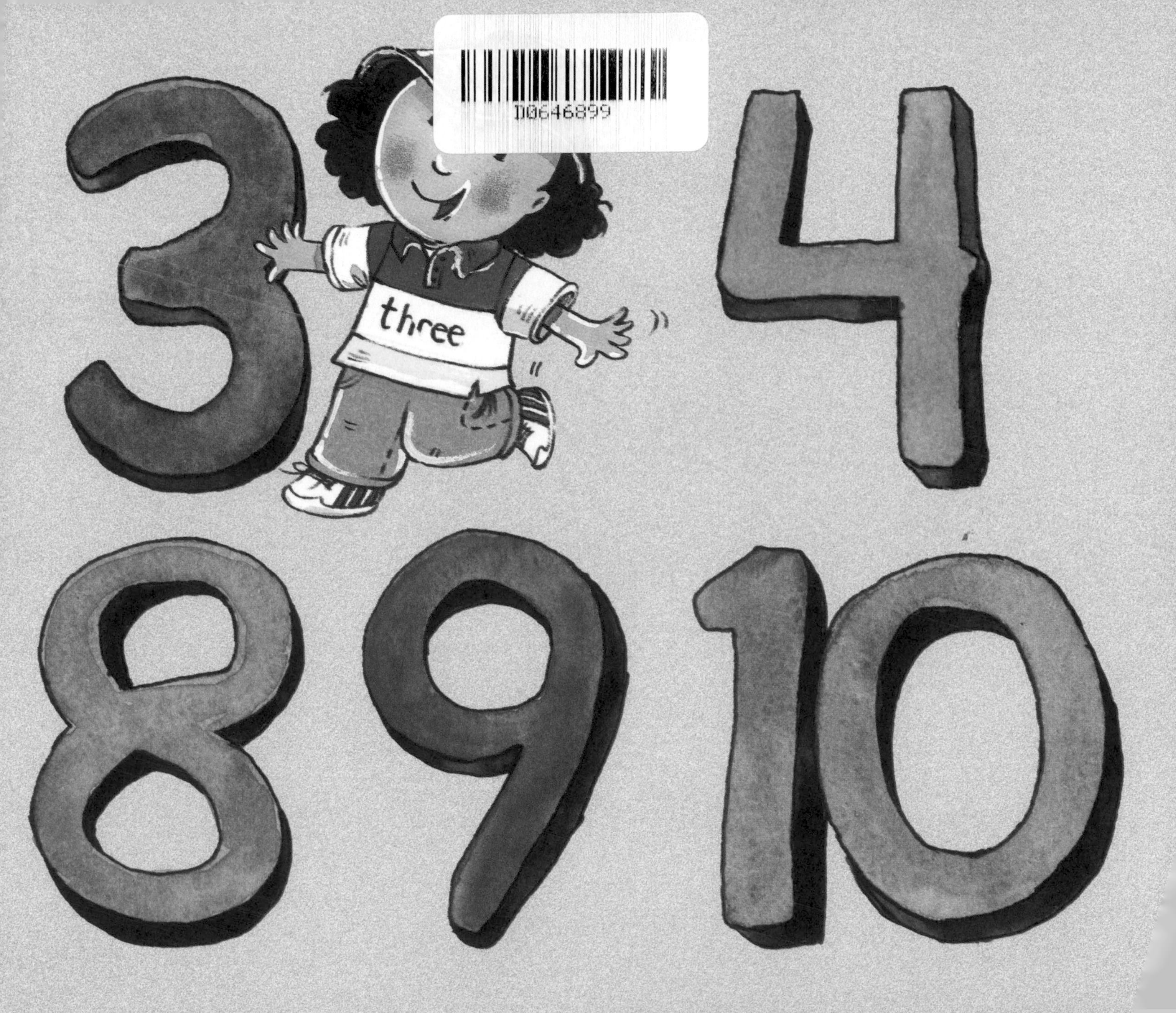
three

Published by Scholastic Inc.,
90 Old Sherman Turnpike, Danbury, Connecticut 06816.

SCHOLASTIC and associated logos are trademarks
and/or registered trademarks of Scholastic Inc.

ISBN 0-7172-8610-X

Printed in the U.S.A.

First Scholastic Printing, August 2005

My "three" Book

by
Jane Belk Moncure

illustrated by
Rusty Fletcher

SCHOLASTIC INC.

New York   Toronto   London   Auckland   Sydney
Mexico City   New Delhi   Hong Kong   Buenos Aires

This is Little three .

She lives in the house of three.

The house of three has three rooms.
Count them.

It has three windows and three
hanging baskets.

Every day Little  three leaves the house to go for a walk.

She jumps three jumps. Can you?

One day Little  three finds three little pigs but . . .

the three little pigs are sad.

"We have lost our houses," they say.
"I will help you," says Little three.

Little  three finds . . .

a house of straw  for the first pig,

a house of wood  for the second pig,

and a house of bricks  for the third pig.

The three little pigs are so happy

that they dance a jig.

Now Little  three finds three bears.

The three bears are sad.
"We have lost our chairs," they say.

So Little  finds . . .

a little chair ,

a middle-sized chair,

and a BIG chair .

How many chairs did she find?

The three bears are so happy!
One dances, one plays a drum,

and one blows a horn.

Little 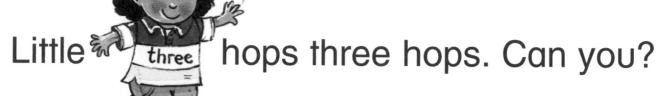 hops three hops. Can you?

She finds one little billy goat, and . . .

then she sees two more billy goats.

How many billy goats does she see?

Away go the three billy goats—

trip, trip, trip—

over the bridge.

Then Little  finds three little mice.

The three mice are sad. They cannot
see very well.

So Little  takes them to the . . .

eye doctor.

She buys them new glasses.
How many pairs does she buy?

The mice are so happy.
The first one stands
on his head.

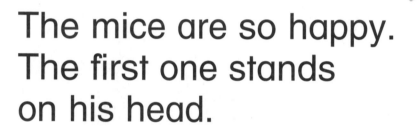

The second
one hops.

The third one
plays a flute.

Little  three plays the fiddle . . .

and the three mice dance.
One, two, three. One, two, three.

Little  finds a . . .

birthday cake and three candles.

Little  says, "This is my birthday."

She blows out the candles.

One, two, three.

Little  three cuts the cake into . . .

three pieces.

One, two, three.

26

She eats two pieces of cake.

Guess what? She leaves one piece of cake for you!

Little  found three of everything.

three
pigs

three
houses

three
bears

three
chairs

three billy
goats

three
glasses

three
mice

three pieces
of cake

Now you find three things.

"See what I can do," says Little .
She makes a 3 this way:

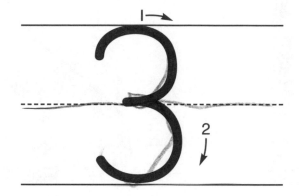

Then she makes the number word like this:

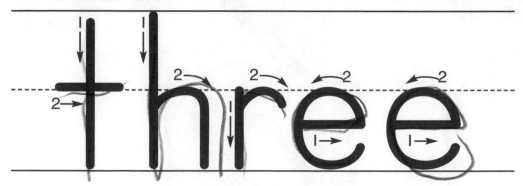

You can make them in the air with your finger.

1 2
5 6 7